THIS JOURNAL
belongs to

_____

Ellie Claire™ Gift & Paper Expressions
Brentwood, TN 37027
EllieClaire.com

Church Notes & Doodles for Girls Journal
© 2014 by Ellie Claire, an imprint of Worthy Media, Inc.

ISBN 978-1-60936-870-8

All rights reserved. No part of this book may be reproduced in any form without permission in writing from the publisher.

Art by Ellen C. Matkowski
Special thanks to Pinky Starbuckle

Scripture from: The Holy Bible, New International Version®, NIV®. Copyright © 1973, 1978, 1984, 2011 by Biblica, Inc.® Used by permission of Zondervan. All rights reserved worldwide. The New American Standard Bible® (NASB), copyright © 1960, 1962, 1963, 1968, 1971, 1972, 1973, 1975, 1977, 1995 by the Lockman Foundation. The Holy Bible, New Living Translation (NLT), copyright 1996, 2004, 2007 by Tyndale House Foundation. Used by permission of Tyndale House Publishers, Inc., Carol Stream, Illinois 60188. *The Message* (MSG). Copyright © 1993, 1994, 1995, 1996, 2000, 2001, 2002. Used by permission of NavPress Publishing Group. *The Living Bible* (TLB) copyright © 1971 by Tyndale House Foundation. Used by permission of Tyndale House Publishers, Inc., Carol Stream, Illinois 60188. All rights reserved.

Printed in China

1 2 3 4 5 6 7 8 9 – 19 18 17 16 15 14

Mfr: R.R. Donnelley / Shenzhen, China / December 2013 / PO # 087221

God must've had a blast.
Painting the stripes on the zebra,
hanging the stars in the sky,
putting the gold in the sunset.

What creativity.

Max Lucado

We should love one another.
1 John 3:11 NLT

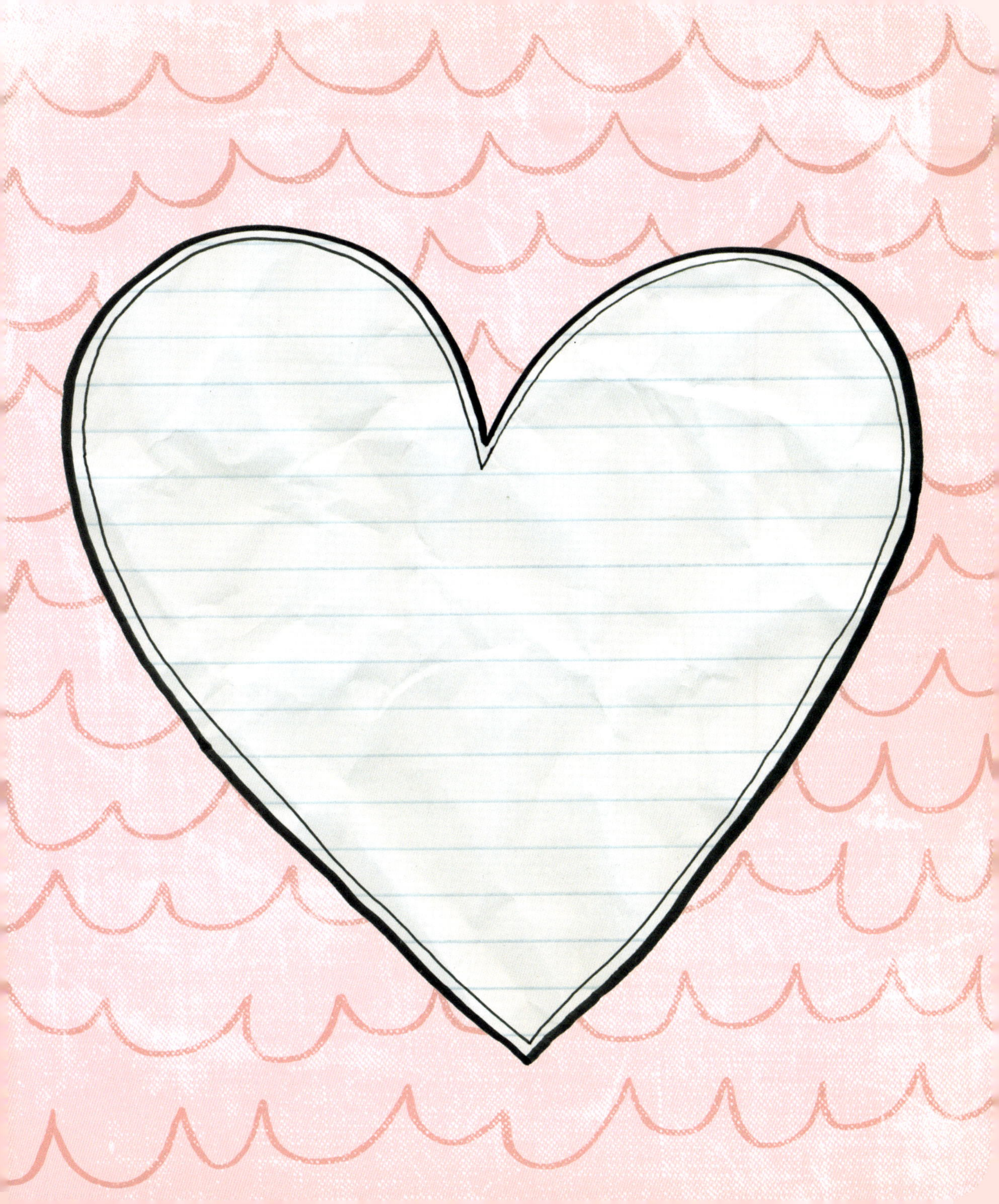

WHAT'S YOUR FAVORITE CANDY?

Date:

O Taste and see that the Lord is GOOD.
Psalm 34:8 NASB

NOTES

> The Lord God took the man and put him in the Garden of Eden to work it and take care of it.
> Genesis 2:15 NIV

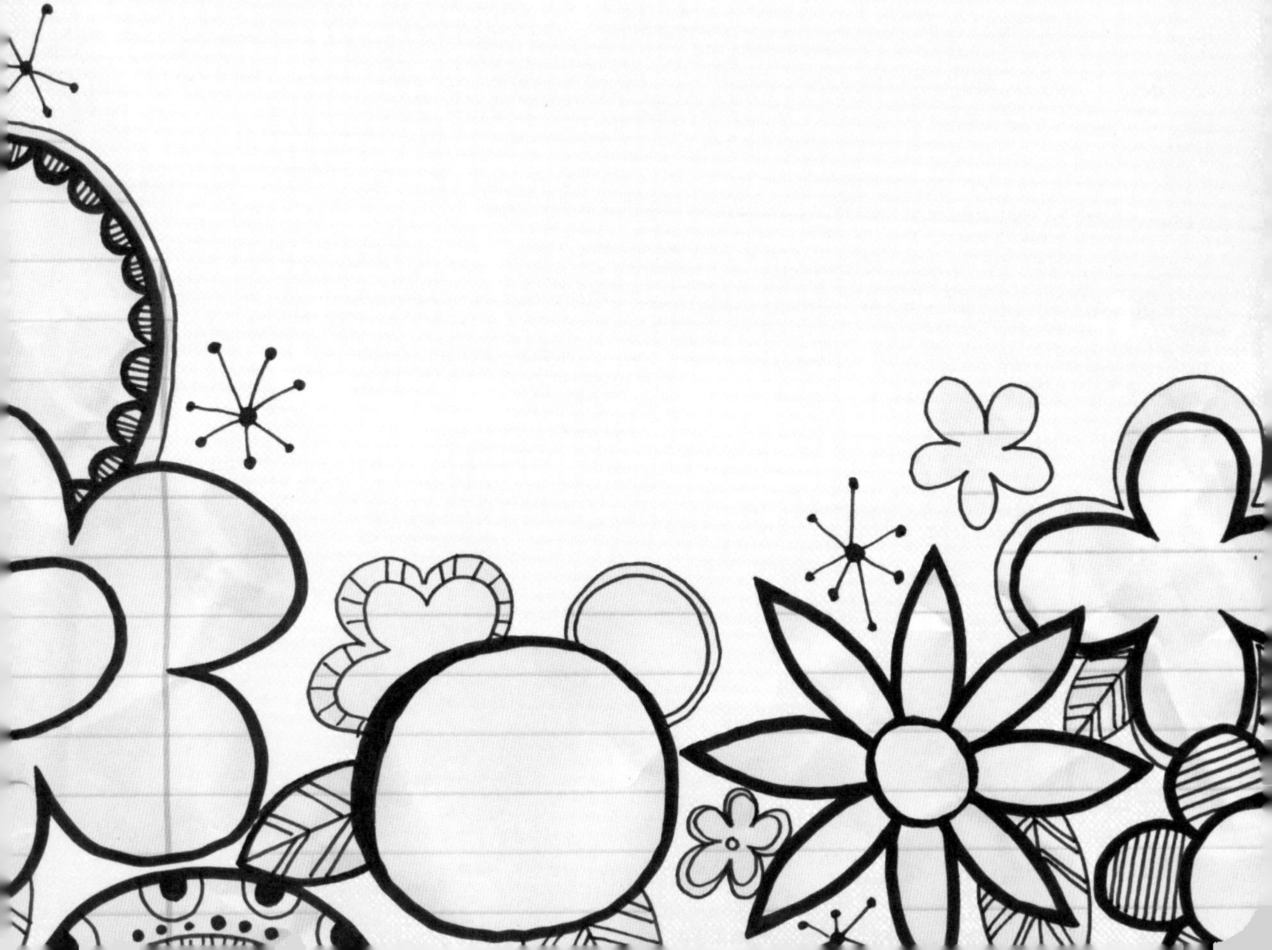

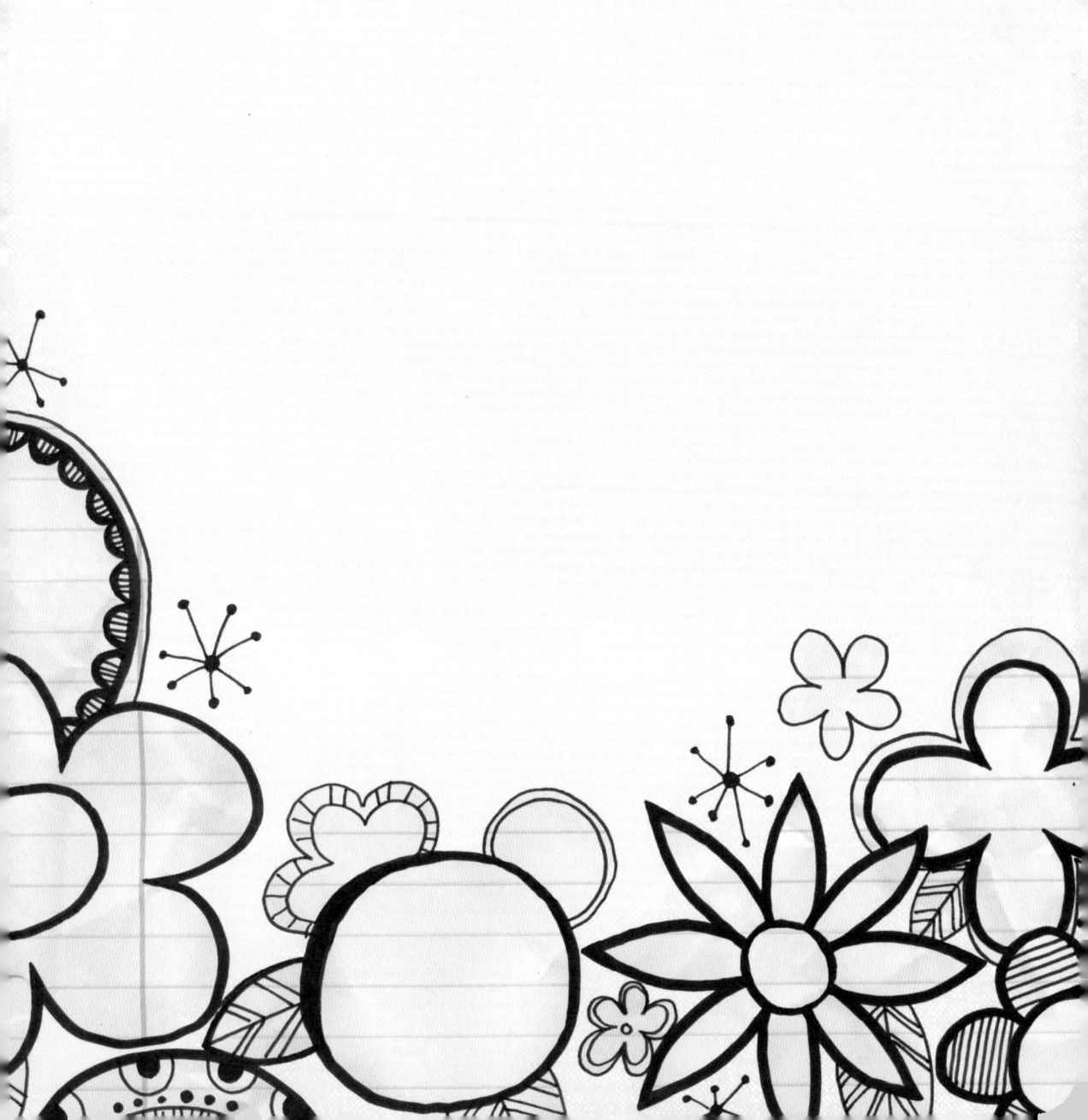

DATE:

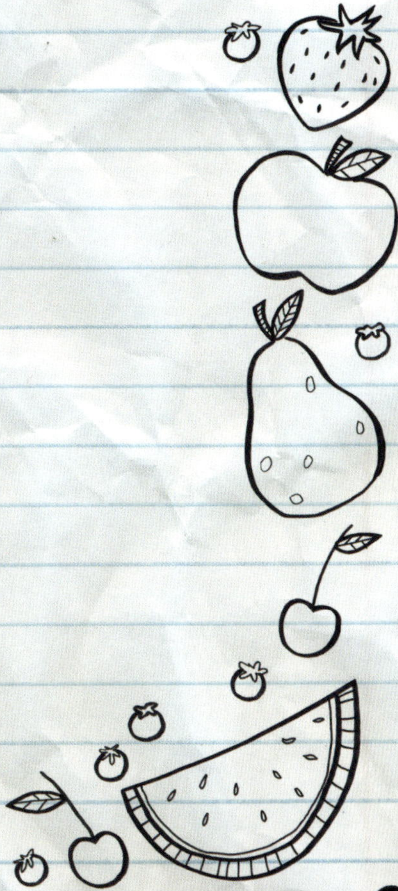

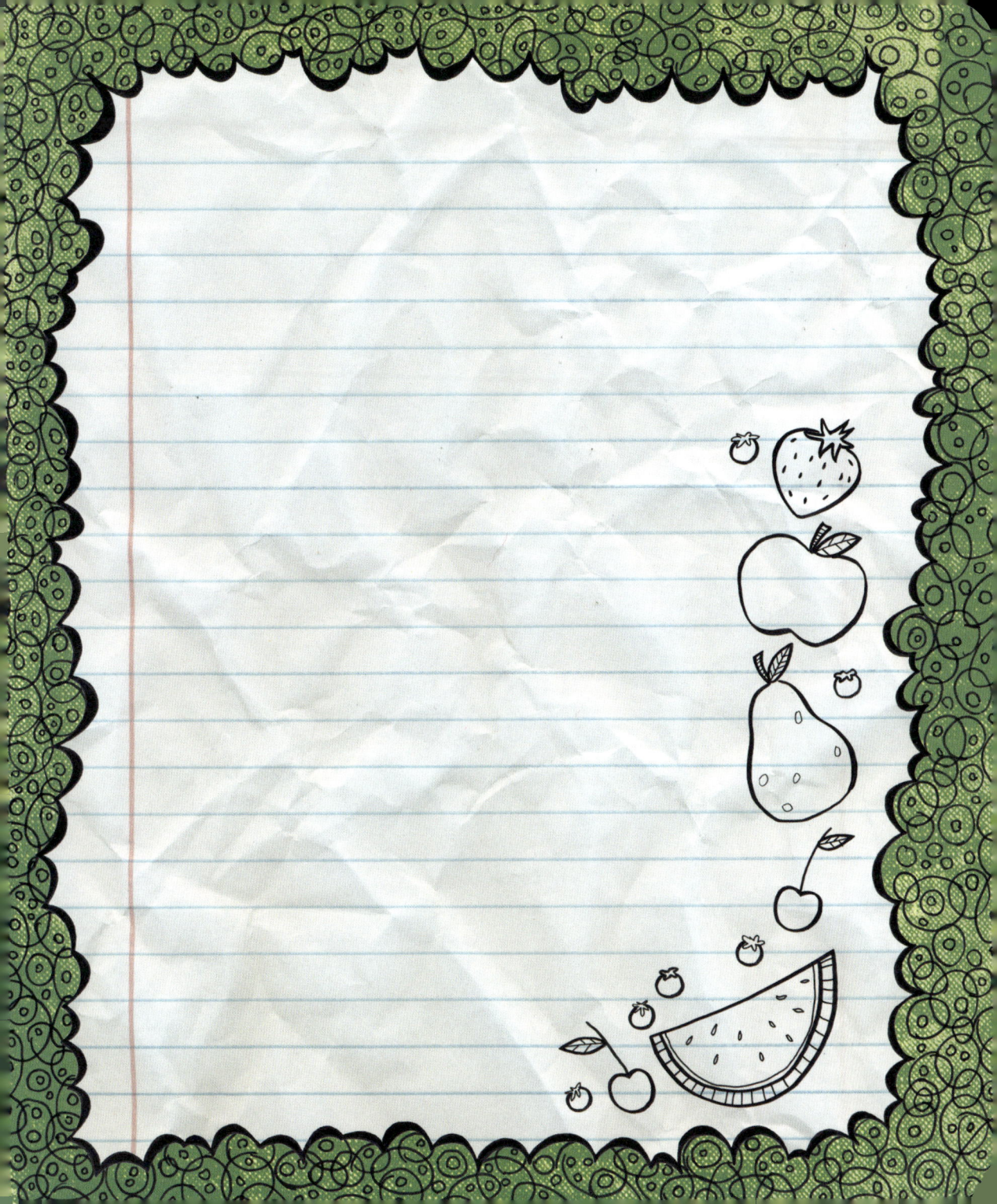

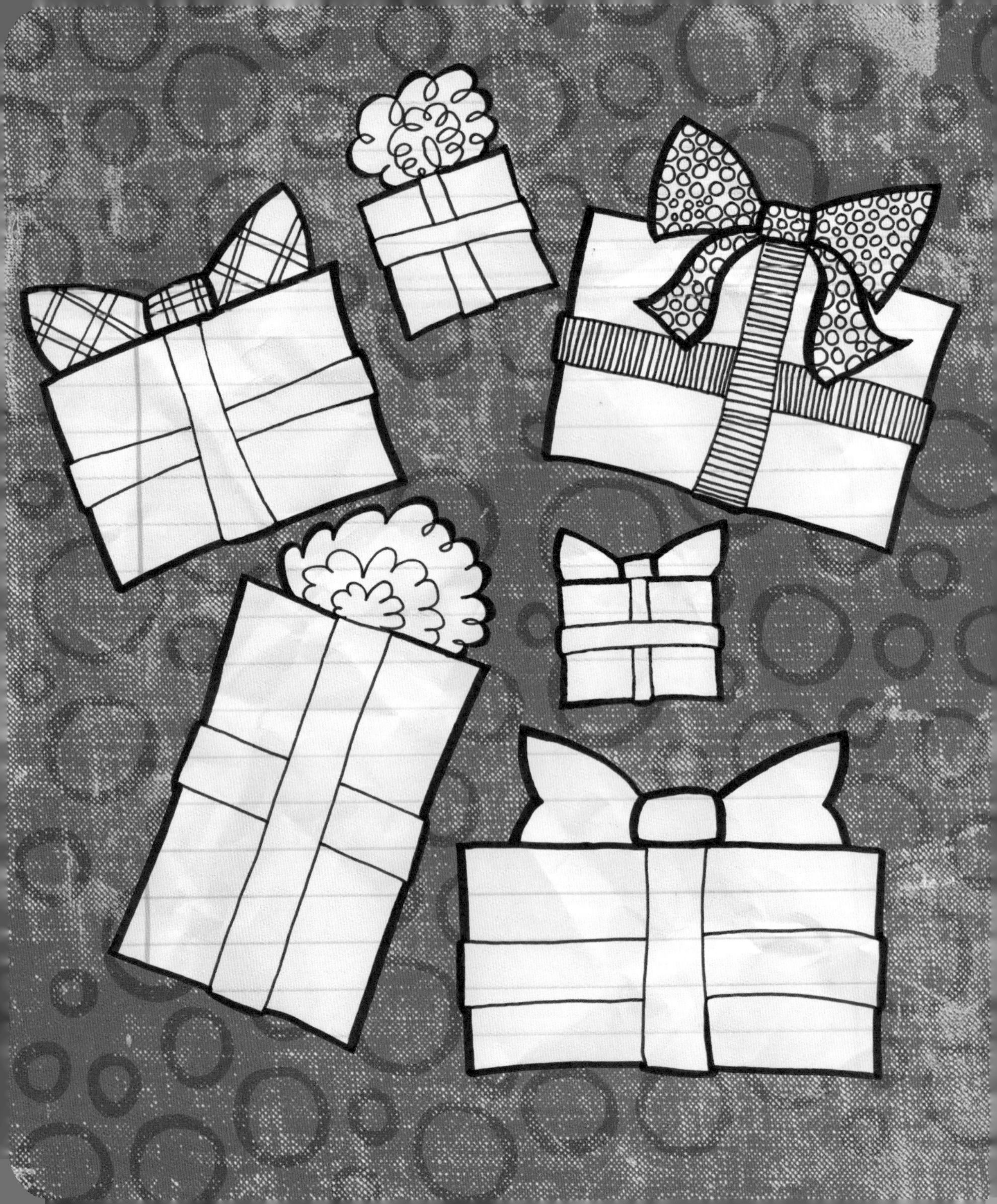

DATE:

God has given each of you a gift from his great variety of spiritual gifts.
1 Peter 4:10 NLT

Date:

DATE:

God created animals with all kinds of wild skin, fins, and fur.

How would you design a fish?

Notes

"Come, follow me," Jesus said, "and I will send you out to fish for people."
Matthew 4:19 NIV

Jesus is from the family of David.
Who are the people in your family?

Notes

God uses interesting patterns in nature.

DATE:

Fabulous Hairstyles!

DATE:

The LORD is good to all.
Psalm 145:9 NIV

People in the Bible wore robes.

What are your favorite clothes?

DATe:

David was dressed
in a robe of fine linen.
1 Chronicles 15:27 NLT

What would you like to juggle?

DATE:

Date:

DATE:

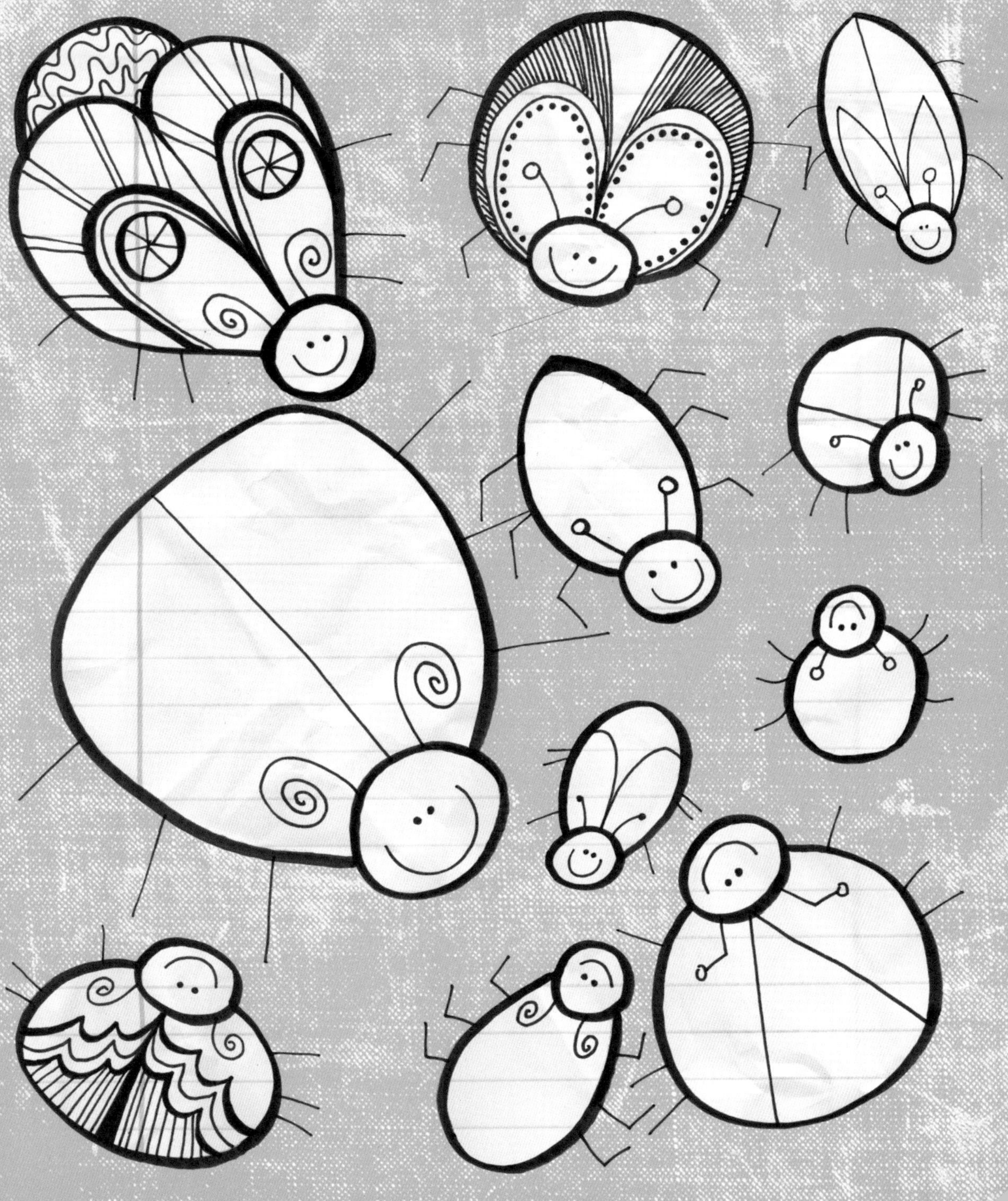

Animal Tracks

NOTES

What do YOU use to CREATE?

DATE:

Notes

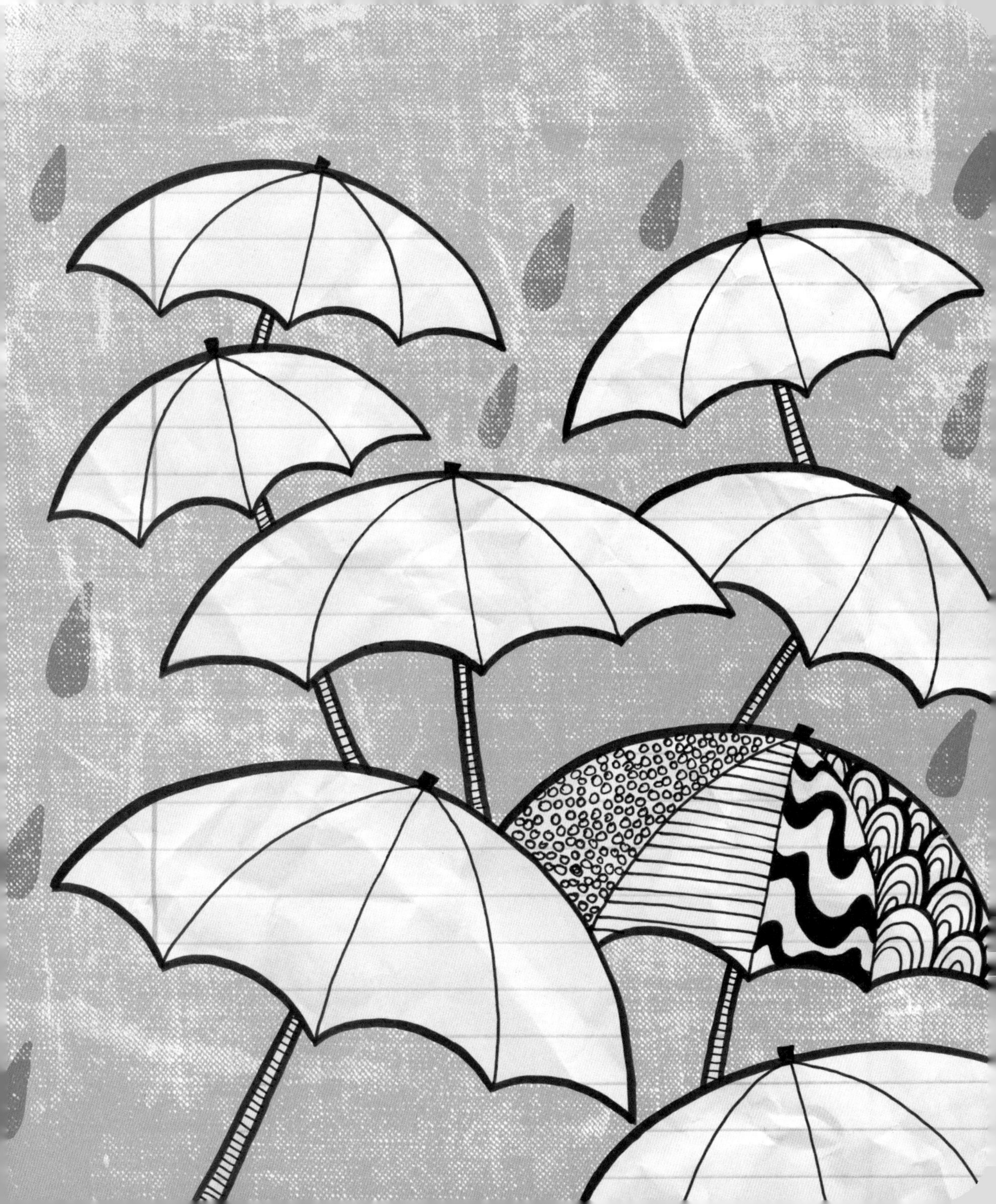

What does your alphabet soup spell?

hi there

DATE:

Date:

In the Bible, people traveled by camel.

How would you like to travel?

DATe:

Write a poem about JESUS.

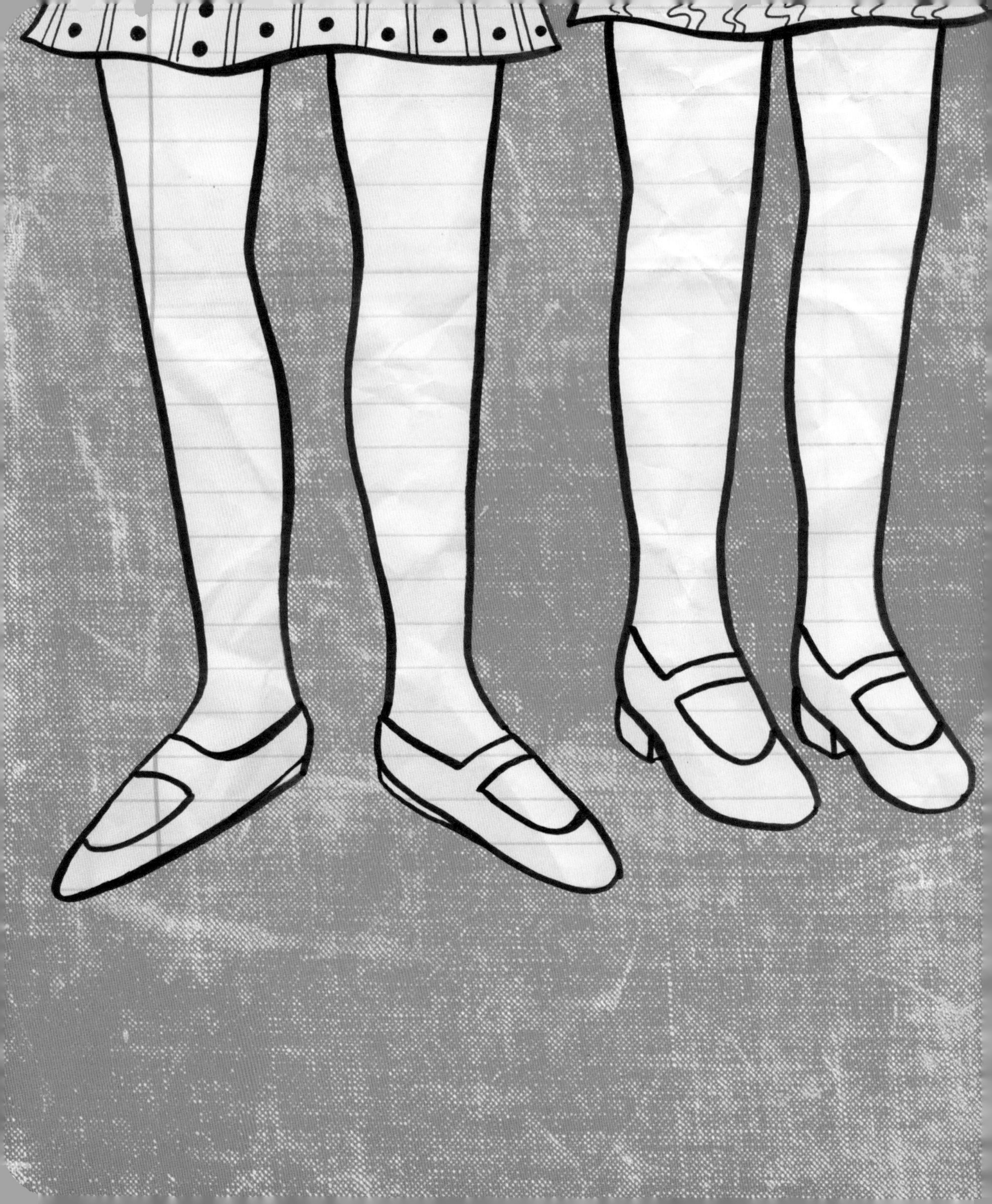

DATE:

Jesus is the LIGHT of the world.

Notes

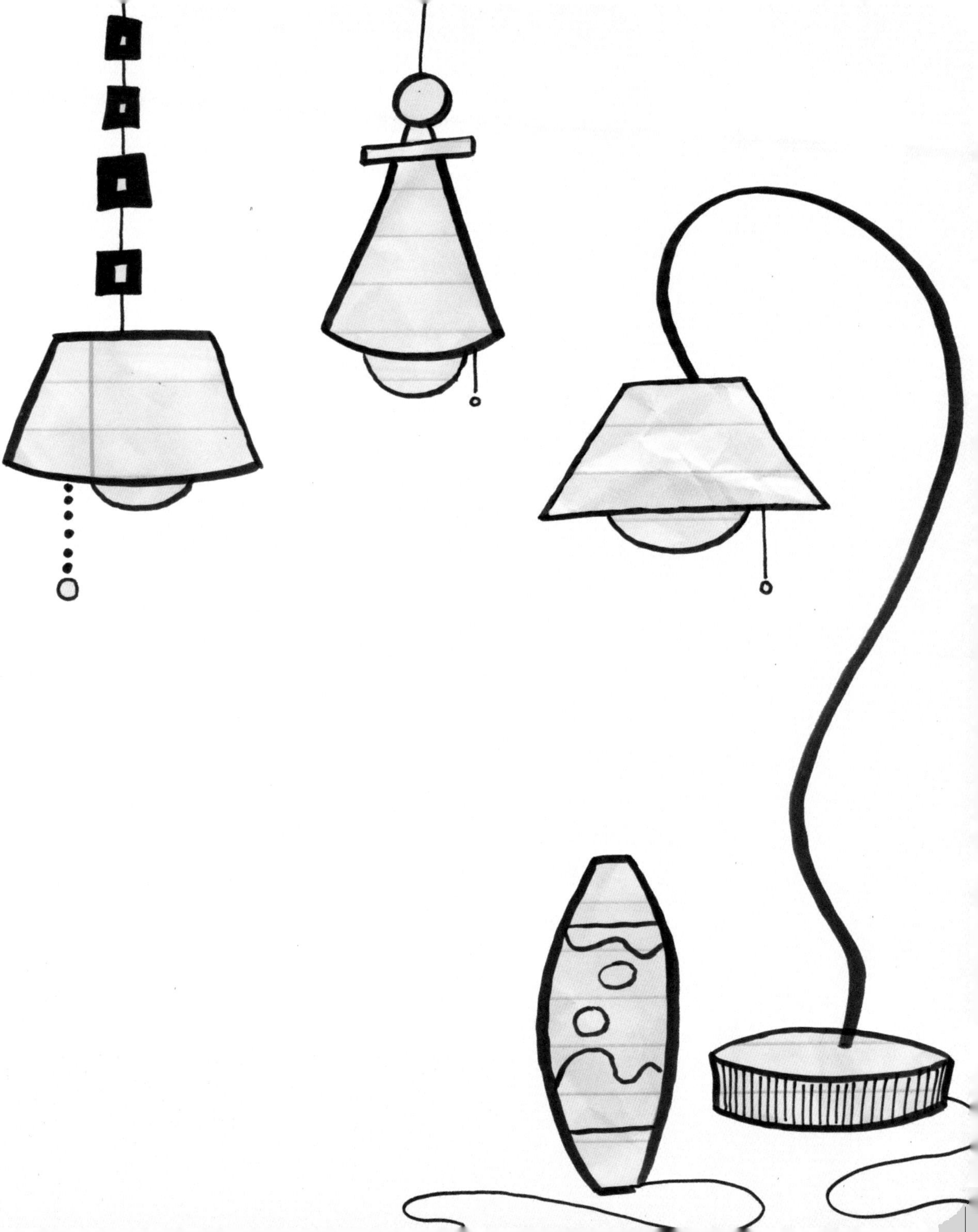

Wow! Fireworks!

DATE:

Date:

NOTES

Father Abraham had many sons and daughters.

How many can you draw?

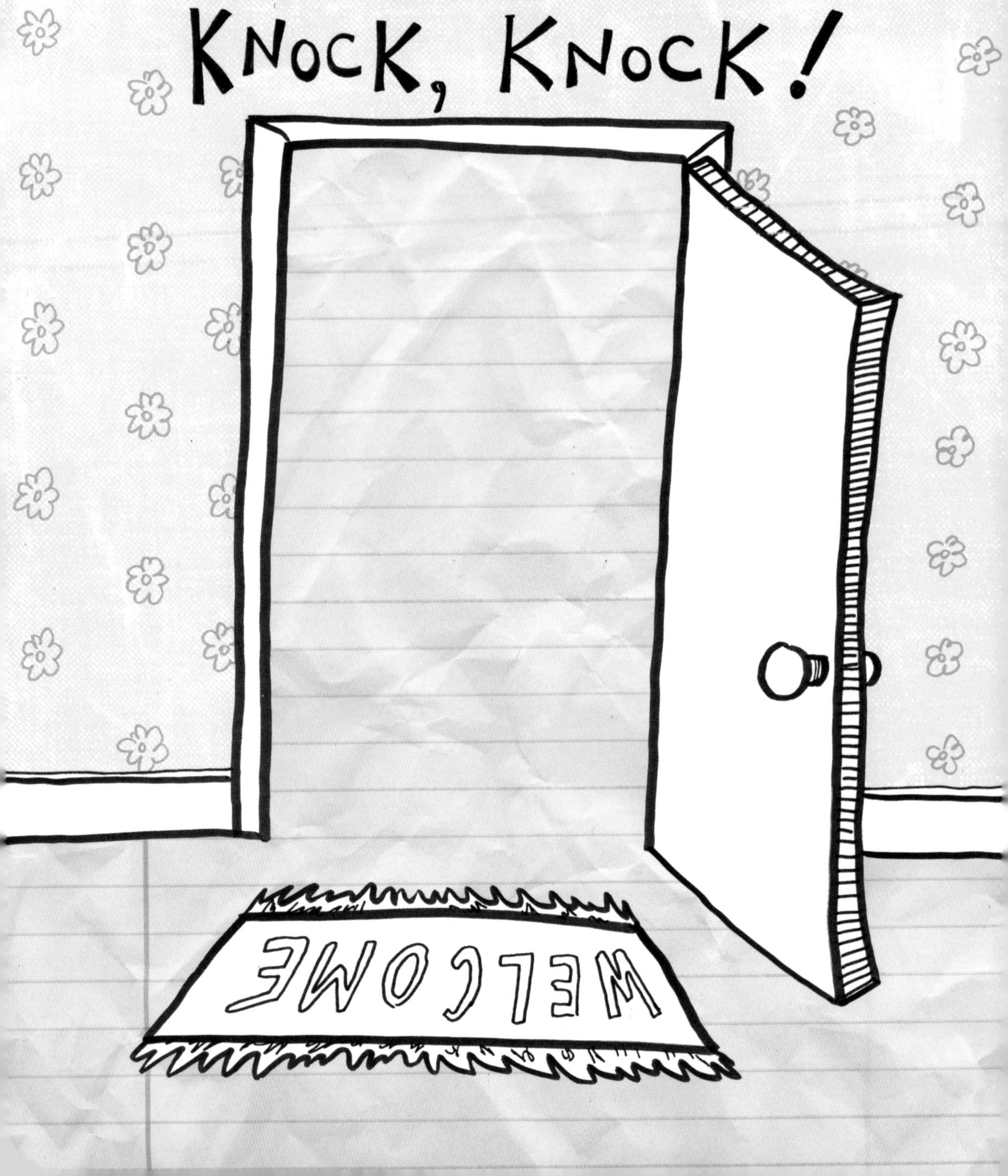
KNOCK, KNOCK!
WELCOME

DATE:

I (Jesus) stand at the door and knock. If you hear my voice and open the door, I will come in.
Revelation 3:20 NLT

Make a list of your happiest memories.

1.
2.
3.
4.
5.

Notes

Who lives under the sea?

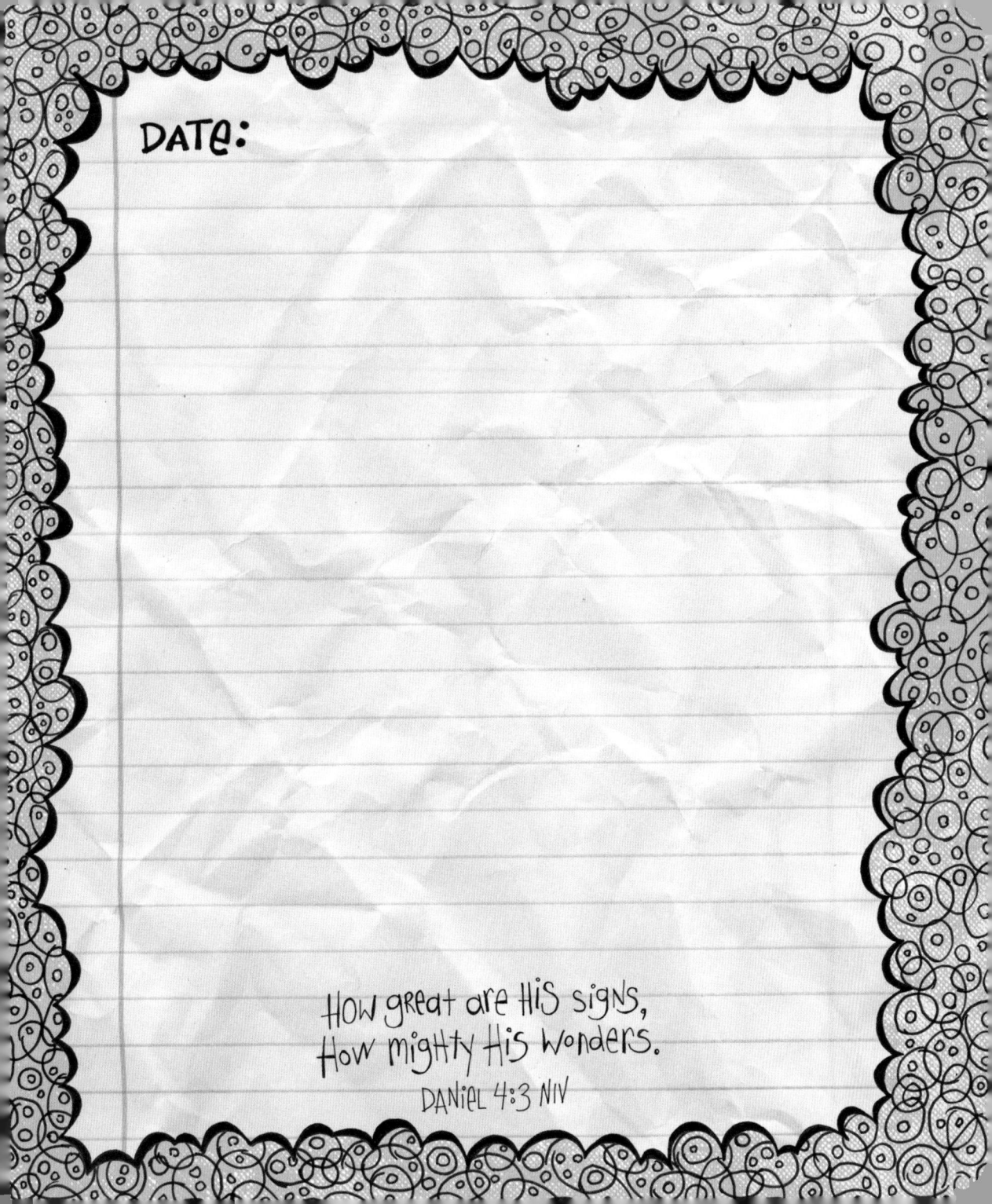

DATE:

How great are His signs,
How mighty His wonders.
 DANIEL 4:3 NIV

Fireflies!

DATE:

Let your LIGHT shine.
MATTHEW 5:16 NIV

Date:

The Bible describes a monster called a **LEVIATHAN**.

Read about the MONSTER in Job 41!

What is your monster's name?

What are you THANKFUL for?

Today I feel like...

DATE:

God filled Noah's Ark with animals.
How many can you think of?

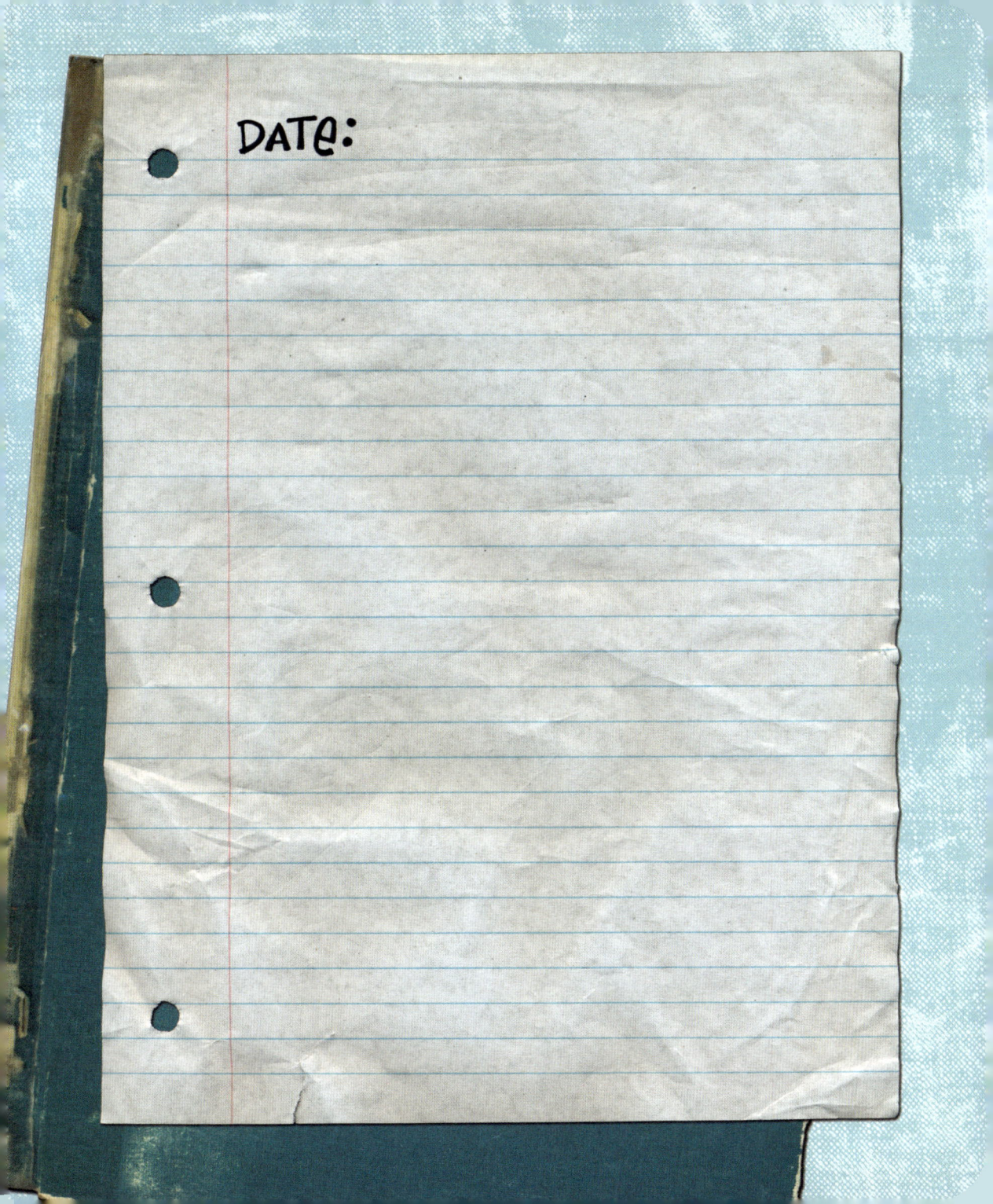

Date:

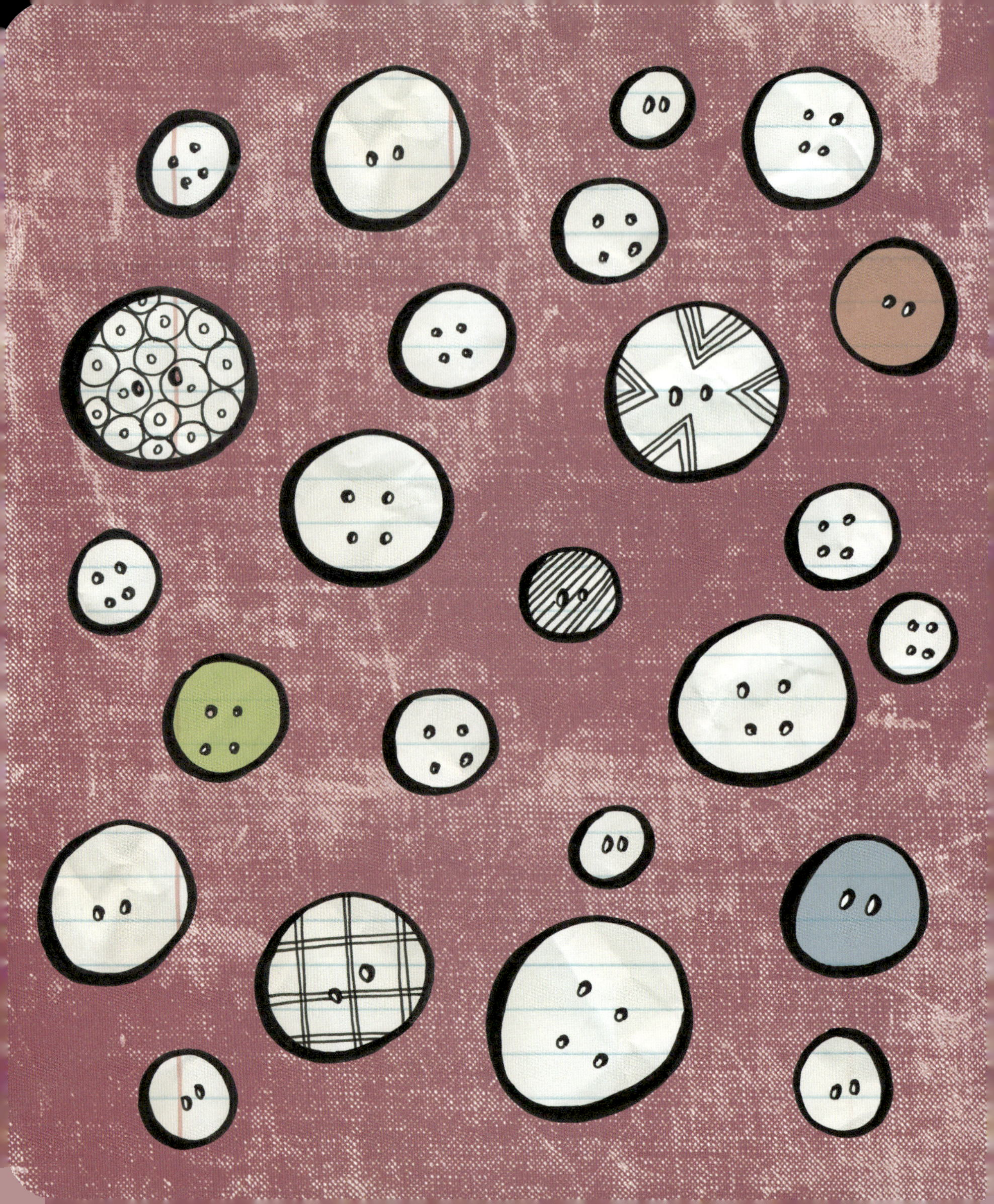

DATE:

Everything, absolutely everything, above and below, visible and invisible... everything got started in Him and finds its purpose in Him.
COLOSSIANS 1:16 MSG

Date:

DATE:

YUM

What is your favorite ice cream treat?

What's for dinner?

← gotta eat your peas!

Date:

Do you wear earrings?

Date:

Adam named all the animals on earth. What names would you make up for new animals?

Date:

> He gave names to all the livestock, all the Birds of the sky, and all the Wild Animals.
> Genesis 2:20 NLT

What are you thinking about?

Date:

DATE:

Notes

Tweet

What sounds do your birds make?

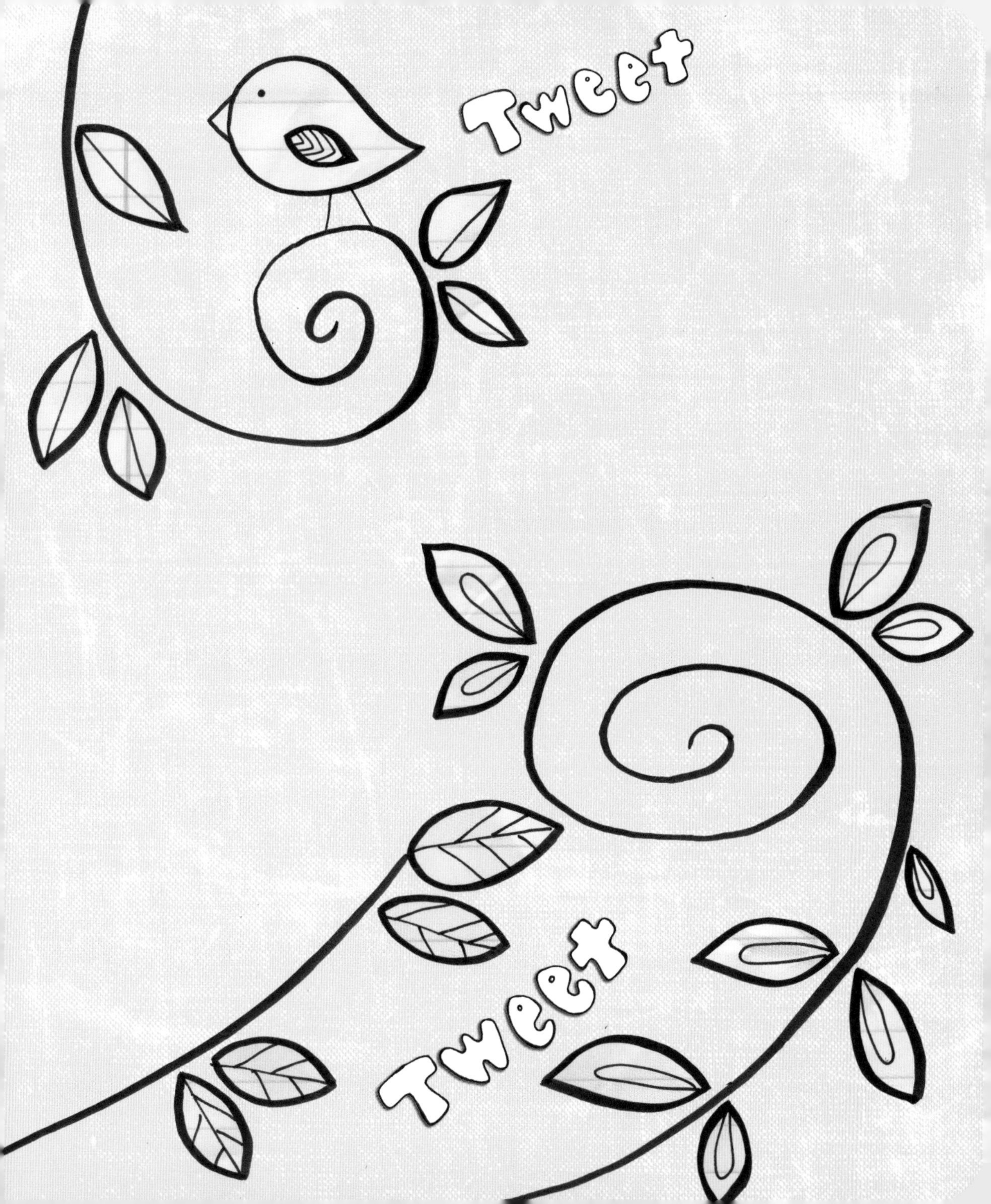
Tweet
Tweet

Jesus was a carpenter.

What would you like to be?

DATE:

> Put GOD in charge of your work
> then what you've planned
> will take place.
> PROVERBS 16:3 MSG

DATE:

Date:

DATE:

TICKETS

DATE:

MY CHILDREN, listen to ME, for all who follow my ways are joyful.
Proverbs 8:32 NLT

Who are your favorite people?

Do to others as you would have them do to you.
Luke 6:31 NIV

God sent manna from heaven.

What food would you like to see fall from heaven?

DATE:

He opened the doors of heaven. He rained down manna for them to eat.

PSALM 78:23-24 NLT

Blessed are those who trust in the Lord.
Jeremiah 17:7 NLT

noTes

NOTES

It's FUN to Dress up!
(but it is what's on the inside that counts.)

My Dream Dress

Be beautiful inside, in your hearts.
1 Peter 3:4 TLB

DATE:

His compassions never fail.
They are NEW every morning;
Great is your faithfulness.
  LAMENTATIONS 3:22-23 NASB

If you had a snowglobe, what would be in it?

Date:

Date:

Notes

God's banner over me is love.
(Song of Songs 2:4)

Methuselah lived a total of 969 years.
(Genesis 5:27)

If he had a cupcake for every year, that would be a LOT.

Date:

You are a princess of God the King!

WHAT KIND OF TIARA WOULD YOU LIKE TO WEAR?

Up Up and Away

Notes

notes

Quilts feel safe and warm.

Date:

The Bible says,
"Pray for each other."
(JAMES 5:16)

1.
2.
3.
4.
5.

Write a list of people you want to pray for.

NOTES

Date: